WICCA
HERBAL MAGIC

A GUIDE TO THE USE OF HERBS AND PLANTS IN WICCAN RITUALS
FOR THE SOLITARY PRACTITIONER,HERBAL SPELLS, HERBAL MAGIC,
CANDLE MAGIC & MOON MAGIC GUIDE

AMY LISA KRYSTAL

Wicca Herbal Magic

A Guide to the Use of Herbs and Plants in Wiccan Rituals for the Solitary Practitioner. Herbal Spells, Herbal Magic, Candle Magic & Moon Magic Guide

Author name

Amy Lisa Crystal

Table of Contents

Introduction

Congratulations on your purchase of *book Wicca Herbal Magic* and thank you for investing in it.

Realizing the power of plants and what they can do in terms of herbal magic is an awakening like few others. You can truly enhance your life in a variety of different ways when you decide to delve into the world of herbs.

This book is going to provide you with an amazing amount of information. It includes information on the roots of herbalism, as well as where you should start with herbs. You will gain valuable insight into buying, growing, caring, and storing some of the most popular magical herbs.

Additionally, there will be information on herbal baths, teas, sachets, and essential oils. All of these pieces play a role in helping you achieve your wants and needs in life. Herbal teas can also help aid you in your magical practices, and we will review some great teas for divination, energy, luck, and prosperity.

No Wicca herbal magic book would be complete without spells. You will have access to a variety of different spells made for beginners. There are spells for success, money, luck, love, health, and more!

Not only will you have access to spells, but you will also gain information on different types of magical boosters that can be used in your herbal spells. The information will include candles, crystals, stones, gems, and meditation. Enhancing the power of your spells does not need to be a difficult process.

Herbal remedies can be more beneficial than prescription medication. Obviously, going natural is a lot of people's preference. You can heal through the magical powers of herbs. They can help you with inflammation, infection, immune functions, and so much more.

Lastly, you will be provided with a guide to full-moon magic. The moon holds an incredible amount of power and harnessing it is advantageous. You can predict outcomes and plan your life out with the power the moon holds.

There are plenty of books on this subject on the market, thanks again for choosing this one! Every effort was made to ensure it is full of as much useful information as possible; please enjoy!

Chapter 1: Introduction to Herbalism

Chapter one is going to be full of background information so that you have a solid basis of knowledge of herbalism. It will include the history of herbalism and some of the most influential people in herbalism. Additionally, you will learn why herbs play such a major role in magical practices.

Shamanism also plays a role in herbal magic and is in the roots of Wiccan beliefs. We will love over the information in regard to this.

Lastly, this chapter will provide you with the ability to enhance your communication with plant spirits. This can lead you to more powerful spells that manifest easier than ones you may have tried in the past. Holding a great relationship with nature is going to impact your spell casting practices positively.

To understand herbalism, we need to take a moment and look at what it actually is. When people discuss herbalism, they are talking about the use of plants or extracts from plants that are used for folk medicines, as well as traditional medicine. A person who becomes well versed in plants and their healing attributes is known as an herbalist. It takes time to learn the information, but once you have it, it opens a lot of doors to lead a healthier and more natural lifestyle.

Herbalism, like everything else, has changed a lot over the course of time. What we see in today's world is not what we would have seen in times of old; however, there will always be similarities. So, how did we get to where we are today with herbalism?

The practice of working with herbs has been seen across the globe for, basically, ever. It is hard to tell you exactly where it all started, as it has always been a thing. There is evidence showing that people of the Paleolithic era practiced herbalism. As you can see, that is an exceptionally long time ago. Herbalism really does run from the bottom of our roots. It is important to note that herbs being used in this timeframe could have been looked at as food rather than being used for their healing and magical properties.

As time marched forth, the use of herbs only became more popular. The first recorded practice of using herbs came from the Shamans around 30,000 BCE. Shamans are keepers of healing and medicine within a variety of different tribes. Shamans were known for their connection to the earth and the spirits of plants. They were said to have the ability to communicate with higher powers. These higher powers would help guide them on how they needed to heal their people. Frequently, this was accomplished with herbal remedies and medicines.

The shamans used cave drawings to record their herbal practices. The first dated records of herbalism happened on clay tablets. They were etched into them by the Sumerians of Mesopotamia. Around the same time, Chinese medicine was also being written down, and it involved a plethora of herbs and plants. You would also find these teachings in India where they were not recorded but past down verbally between an herbalist teacher to their student.

Around the same period, the Egyptians were also starting to compile written information on the healing properties of herbs and plants. They compiled a variety of different medical texts that helped to describe herbs, their properties, and their uses. Some of the information they provided is still held in high regard today.

As time continued, herbs played a significant role in medicine and healing. Whether looking at the perspective of Christians or Pagans, the power of herbs cannot be denied. There were times that people looked at herbalism as witchcraft, and it was shunned; however, it never really stopped. People have consistently practiced the art of herbalism for generations, and that is never going to stop.

Herbs have always played a role in magic. Let's face it; plants have been a part of this world much longer than humans have. This is why many people can easily understand why herbs and plants are a great tool in your arsenal of magical items.

The properties of herbs are known to be able to help us heal both physically and spiritually. There are so many different plants, and they all hold different properties that can be utilized during magical workings. There was a time that medicine and magic went hand in hand. It was not only about the herbs but also about the rituals and mantras that were used to ensure someone was truly on the path of healing.

In today's world, there is a separation between medicine and magic; however, that is not the case for everyone. Many can plainly see how they work together for powerful effects. When you combine magical herbs with spells, rituals, and incantations, the results are astounding. That is why herbs will always play a major role in magical endeavors.

Herbs & Magic

Herbs and plants also play a role in Wiccan practices due to the fact that they are associated with the elements. Herbs and plants encompass the four main elements. They are grown from the earth, nourished by the sun and rain, and they provide us with oxygen. They interact with the elements in more ways than just this; however, it gives you a glimpse at the correlation between plants and the elements. Each and every plant cover all of the four major elements we come into contact with.

From ancient times, all the way to today, there is a belief that plants have a soul or a spirit. Philosophers, Wiccans, and witches all agree that this statement is very true. Surprisingly, there are actually a large number of scientists that also believe in the consciousness of plants.

This consciousness allows plants to connect with not only each other but also with us. There is proof that plants will work together to help the other foliage around them. They do this with their root systems. Nutrients can be exchanged from one plant to another. If one plant, tree, or shrub is lacking in a certain area, others will help it out to ensure its survival.

Interestingly enough, they can also help warn each other about predators. A good example of this comes with bugs that eat leaves. When a bug starts chomping on a leaf, plants will release chemicals to inform the other plants that they need to do the same. This release of chemicals is for duel purposes. In addition to warning the other plants of a predator, it also helps repel the insect from the plant it is currently eating.

All of these things help to show how smart plants are and the type of power that they hold. Witches and Wiccans will use this power to energize their spellcasting and help manifest a variety of different wants, needs, and desires. It doesn't matter what part of the plant you are working with; it can hold the key to success in spellcasting.

When it comes to magic, plants and herbs are exceptionally versatile. They are connected with the earth and can provide you with the earth's energy. It is best to grow and use your herbs as you can charge them with the appropriate energy as you grow and cultivate them. Growing them, yourself will also provide you with hands-on access to the energies of all four of the main elements; earth, air, fire, and water.

Herbs are used in a large variety of different spells. You can create spell jars, poppets, pillows, sachets, and various other charms with them. It is also common for people to make essential oils and incense with them. This can provide you with higher levels of magical energy and more power for your spells.

The use of herbs in witchcraft is commonly seen. From spells involving candles or crystals to purification and blessings, herbs can help provide long-lasting results. Herbs are used in different cultures and traditions. This is due to the simple fact that they hold a lot of power, and their uses have been proved time and time again.

There is a plethora of information available about herbs and how to use them in your magical practices. It can seem daunting at first. Understand that with time, study, and dedication, it will become easier. Later in this book, we will look at some of the must-have herbs to conduct spells, rituals, incantations, and other magical workings. You will be provided with a good amount of basic knowledge so you can start working with herbs right away.

Pioneers of Herbalism

While the roots of herbalism run deep, there are a few people that helped pave the way for its popularity and practical use. Realistically, there are a large number of people that played a role; however, some were more important than others. Understanding the pioneers of herbalism will help give you a solid foundation for the reasons that herbalism is still so important and widely used today.

One of the first names that need to be mentioned in herbalism pioneers is Hippocrates. His famous quote, "Let your food be your medicine and let your medicine be your food," is exceptionally famous and gives us some of the first insights into how healing the use of herbs and plants can be. He helped people understand that herbs are critical to our existence and our health.

Hippocrates was not exceptionally spiritual. He was much more logical. The remedies that he used for herbal healing were akin to the ones the Shamans used. He did not use herbs and plants in combination with prayers, rituals, and rites, but he did use them for healing and providing healthier lives to those around him. His lack of spirituality is what truly separates him from Shamans and witches.

Galen of Pergamon was a Greek physician and also a pioneer of herbalism. He did his best to document all of the medical knowledge that he had. This included a variety of works that discussed herbs, plants, and their perspective properties.

One of his most famous books combined the use of herbs within medicine to not only make people healthier but also help with preventative measures. His knowledge and books helped medical workers calibrate medicines so that they worked for each person individually. It helped show that each person is unique and needed to be dealt with in an individualized manner.

Nicholas Culpeper is another name that goes hand in hand with the words herbal pioneer. He lived a short life but was frequently referred to as "the People's Herbalist." The impact that he had on the world of herbology is outstanding. For as influential as he was, his peer group did not accept him due to his viewpoints and beliefs in areas like Astrology.

Culpeper was a doctor that had a passion for helping those that were less fortunate. He spent most of his time studying and writing down properties and information on plants and herbs. There are many books published by him that were then translated into a variety of different languages. These books are still being used today and have given the ability to use herbal remedies to a plethora of people from the moment they were written.

Due to the fact that he lived a life of struggles, he had a true appreciation and desire to help those that were underprivileged. Not only did he provide medical services for little to no cost, but he also advised people on what they could do to become healthier. The people that sought his services truly loved him because he dedicated his life to helping those that were in need regardless of their financial standing.

Culpeper wanted to let people know they could heal through natural methods. He took his knowledge of the pharmaceutical industry and combined it with his research on plants and herbs to provide people with options and information on health and healing. The collection of books he had published was massive. They are still studied and used in the world today.

There was a period of time that natural healing through herbs was less than popular; however, it has always been around and always will be. The Council on Medical Education was founded by the American Medical foundation, and it helped in the downfall of herbalism for a while. This group removed herbalism from classes and many medical schools. The popularity of herbalism declined due to the lack of information that was available to students.

Herbalism's popularity has started to flourish again. The healthy solutions that herbs offer will ensure they are never taken completely off the table. Many people want to heal naturally and believe it leads to a better and more fulfilled life. The information on herbs and their healing power is much more readily available in today's society and will continue to be around regardless of the level of popularity.

While we have only looked at a few of the herbal pioneers of the world, it is important to understand that many others played their part. We will continue to grow and learn about herbs and plants, so; herbal pioneers will continue to be a thing. Just because this is a practice of old does not mean that it will not continue to evolve and change. As it does, people will continue to impact it and become critical in the expansion of herbal knowledge.

Communication with Plant Spirits

Earlier, it was mentioned that plants have a spirit or a soul. We have the ability to communicate with them, believe it or not. In the past, it was a common practice for shamans to connect with higher powers by way of plants. It helped align them with the spirit world.

We were all once truly connected to the earth and nature. In today's world, it is less common, but it can be achieved. The spirituality of the shamans and their connection to plants lives on today through folklore. Many healers, witches, and herbalists believe that our ailments come from disruptions in our emotional and spiritual bodies. Plants are known for being strong healers in these areas.

By building a good relationship with nature, plants, and herbs, we can regain our ability to heal with them naturally. These teachings may not be as prominent as they used to be; however, they are certainly making a comeback. More people are finding healthier and more fruitful lives by connecting to things that are natural rather than manmade.

Not only do many people believe that we can speak to plants, but also that they can speak to us. If we listen closely, we can hear them calling. If you want to start listening for the call of nature, the best thing you can do is get out and experience it. Taking the time to go for a hike in a secluded part of the wilderness is a great way to do this.

As with all things magical, you need to set your intention and hold it in focus as you wander around a natural setting. This intention will help the right energies find you. Once you start to hear the call of the plants that surround us, you will be more likely to understand their powerful energy and healing properties.

When you are trying to enhance your connection with herbs and other plants, you need to not only have a focused intent but also provide an offering. Plants will work with you if they feel you are worthy. By providing them with an offering such as nutrients, you will find they are more likely to offer you information on healing and their other attributes.

Another way to connect with the spirit of plants more easily is to ensure you treat them with respect. By loving and respecting plants, they will be more likely to want to communicate with you. Many understand that plants have feelings, so when we show them respect, compassion, and love, it makes sense that they will want to work with us to heal and brighten the spirits and minds around them.

Meditation in nature is another great way to connect with plants and their spirits. Focused meditation will allow you to take in your surroundings truly and can make it easier to hear what it is that the plants and herbs around you are trying to say. This takes time, patience, and practice. Know that with continued focus, love, and intention, connection with plant spirits can become quite easy.

Chapter 2: Beginning the Path with Herbs

Chapter two will provide you with insight into where you should begin with herbs. We will discuss buying herbs versus growing them yourself or collecting them in the wild. Most people find the most success with spellcasting when they grow their own herbs, but others prefer to purchase them.

You will also learn about how to care for herbs if you are growing them at home or cultivating them in the wild. This includes how to make a garden at home, even if you have limited space. There are some things you need to consider if gathering herbs in the wild and certain herbs or plants you should stay away from; these will be discussed, as well.

Lastly, you can gain a lot of insight on how to gather, dry, and store your herbs. How you handle them will ensure they are ready for use for your magical practices. If handled wrong, you can cause detriment to the energy; they hold, which can, in turn, negatively impact your spells.

There are a plethora of different plants and herbs that are available to you. Many people find it intimidating in trying to figure out where to start. It does not need to be intimidating, however. There are some basic herbs that every witch or Wiccan should have access to at any point in the day.

Let's start this chapter by looking at ten different herbs that you should always have around. They will enhance your spellcasting and magical practices. Many of them, you will likely already have at home while others you may need to start growing or invest in.

Keep in mind that growing your own herbs or collecting them in the wild is the best way to go. However, if you don't have a green thumb buying them from a store is also acceptable.

Apple blossoms are a great thing to have to lay around. Throughout time apples have been a sign of immortality. Not only is it linked to immortality, but it is also linked to the dead. In some mythical lore, The Apple branch with fruit growing on it can open the gateway to the underworld. Apples are also frequently used for the magic that is used for love. It is also fantastic when making a variety of different brews, incense, and incantations.

Basil is the next herb that you were going to want to have on hand. It holds a lot of different magical properties. It can be used with purification spells and luck spells. Not only that, good fortune can be found when you have a basil plant growing in your home. Basil is a very versatile herb. On top of all of these things, it can be used in love spells and divination. It truly is handy to have available.

If you are searching for an herb that is fantastic for protection, as well as purification, you should look towards chamomile. Many people use it during meditation. It can also be used to protect yourself against psychological or magical attacks. When you work chamomile into your incense, it can be a great benefit if you have been having trouble sleeping. Chamomile is known for bringing good luck. This can be good luck in gambling or when trying to find a lover. In general, this plant can be used to fill your life with good fortune.

Lavender is another herb that is absolutely critical to have on hand. It is oftentimes used in spells that will bring love your way. Additionally, if you are searching for peace or calmness in your life, lavender can help you achieve it. It is used frequently in sachets. You will also find it hanging around people's homes to ensure that they do not suffer from nightmares and that they get a good night's sleep.

Found in many magical practices is the herb Mugwort. It is frequently used in casting spells, for incense, and for smudging. This herb is extremely versatile and simple to grow. You won't need a green thumb to be successful. Working on divination will require the use of this herb. It helps to show us prophecy through our dreams and during meditation. Pregnant women should be mindful when using Mugwort as it may be harmful.

Another popular herb that you should have on hand is Patchouli. It is used in a variety of different spells and rituals. The scent helps to take our minds to other realms. It is connected to spells that are cast for wealth, love, and sexual prowess. Many find that its power is excellent for bringing money into your life. There are a variety of different spells that can be cast with this herb to help you find your way out of financial difficulties. In today's world, it is also good for repelling negativity from our lives.

A plethora of strength and protection spells can be accomplished with the herb, Pennyroyal. Pennyroyal is known to help remove malintent from your life. People frequently make sachets stuffed with this herb for protection. It can easily be carried around with you and Ward off any negative energies that are coming your way. Additionally, it is associated with prosperity and wealth. You can make a variety of different drinks and soaps to help bring money into your life.

Rosemary is another common herb that holds a lot of magical properties in most people already have at home. When you are trying to enhance your memory or improve your brainpower, this herb is a necessity. Rosemary is used in a variety of different religious practices. Many cultures find that it offers a great level of protection from evil spirits. It is frequently burned in the home to remove negative energy. It is also exceptionally helpful during meditation. You will find that your focus is better. Rosemary is also hung on doors to help keep people that would do you harm away.

The next common herb that you will most likely already have at home that we are going to discuss is sage. Sage is fantastic for purification of your home or the cleansing of a space. Burning sage is also frequently used in rituals. In times long since passed, it was used to bring wisdom and clarity to a person's mental status. Carrying sage leaves can help to improve your finances.

Additionally, it can help provide you with guidance from the spirit world. These are only a few of the many uses for sage. It really is one of the most critical herbs to ensure that you have on hand.

Yarrow is another basic herb that is very useful in magical practices. It has great healing potential and can be used in healing spells, as well as a variety of healing ointments. Yarrow is frequently used in spells for love and ones for courage. It can be worn to provide higher levels of self-esteem. Many people use it to help them overcome their fears. Yarrow is used in magical bathing, as well as in sachets.

This is only a glimpse at the herbs that you will want to have in your magical Arsenal. It is a great place to start. You need to understand that there is a large variety of herbs available to you, and while many of them hold similar properties, they are all unique in their own way. Getting to know the most common herbs is advantageous. It will take time, research, and dedication to learn these magical herbs, but at the end of the day, they will truly help you along your path toward leading a healthier and happier life.

Buying Herbs Vs. Growing Herbs

In this section, we're going to take a brief look at the differences between buying herbs and growing them or collecting them yourself. There are a variety of different viewpoints on the best course of action when it comes to how you obtain your herbs. Realistically, growing them or collecting them from the wild is always going to be the best course of action.

When you go into your local grocery store, there is always a decent variety of different plants and herbs that you can choose from. Sometimes this is your only option. The problem with buying your herbs from a store is their energy levels. Additionally, there could be issues and how the plants were handled and raised, which may impact their power when using them for spellcasting.

When a plant is sitting in a store, a variety of different people will come into contact with it. They will imprint some of their energy on to the plant, whether intentional or not. This could lead to negative effects when you go to use it. You can cleanse your herbs to rid them of negative energies if you have decided to buy your herbs from a store. In fact, it is quite critical that you remove any energies that they may have picked up before you start using them.

Since plants are very sensitive, where they're grown will play a role in the power that they hold. If you buy your plants and herbs from a store, it is likely that not much attention was paid to them while they were young and just starting to grow. This could mean that you are working with diminished energy levels. It is possible to charge your herbs and enhance their energy level, and it is likely going to be advantageous to spend the time to do this if you are buying your herbs from a marketplace.

There are specialized stores that you can buy live or dried herbs from. These specialized stores will often focus on witchcraft. If you're buying your herbs from this type of store, you will probably have more success than buying them from your local grocery store. However, be warned that when you are buying herbs from a specialty shop like this, you may end up paying a lot more for them. Additionally, you have to remember that while most people have good intentions, there are people out there with nefarious ones. They could put negative intent into the items that they're selling, and it could affect you in a less than stellar way.

Creating an herb garden in growing your own plants is always the best course of action. You will then be able to not only grow them with love but with intent. The communication between you and the plants around you will be enhanced. They will feel loved, and therefore they will grow stronger an provide you with higher levels of positive energy during spellcasting practices.

You don't have to have the greenest of thumbs to accomplish an herb garden. Herbs are actually relatively simple to grow. In addition, it does not take a large amount of space to create an herb garden. It can be done in small apartments or in large fields. It simply doesn't matter. All you need to do is have the drive and desire to grow your own herbs to make it happen.

If you truly don't want to grow an herb garden, you can also gather them from the wild. You need to be very careful when doing this and make sure that you are solid in what you are looking for. Knowing the shape, size, smell, and locations of where specific herbs grow is very important. If you pick the wrong plant, it could lead to devastating effects. Some herbs and plants look very similar but have very different properties. What you may be using for a healing spell might end up actually harming you because it is a toxic plant, and you did not realize it.

So, if you were going to venture out into the wild, you are going to need to spend time doing some research. First, you will need to look at the plant species that grow around you. Certain plants will only be available in certain areas of the world. You will also need to get to know the plant as a whole. This will make it easier to recognize while you are hunting for it.

Overall, regardless of how you decide to collect your herbs, it is critical that you build a basic foundation of knowledge in regard to them. Knowing their properties and magical uses will help you choose the correct items. You should also learn how to dry them and store them. We are going to look at that in more detail in just a   moment.

Growing Herbs

Growing herbs at home do not need to be a difficult process. It is the most advantageous way to cultivate these magical plants. Learning how to grow them at home is advantageous in manifesting the spells to which you plan on casting. Your garden can be grown inside or outside of your home.

When you decide to create a garden that helps you to connect with nature, in addition, you will feel better and higher connection with your plants. It can help you communicate with them an understand the remedies they can add to your life. You will need to understand how plants grow and what you need to do to ensure that they flourish. Each herb is going to be handled differently, so learning a couple at a time is advantageous so that you do not become overwhelmed.

When you first start to delve into the world of learning how to grow herbs, one of the best things you can do is observe them in their natural habitat. When you start to look at them, it can have a powerful impact. It helps you connect with the plants and also has a very calming effect. When you connect with plants in their natural environment, it will be easier to connect with them once you have them in your home.

Another benefit of observing plants grow in nature is that it can allow you to see what happens in their environment. It can give insight into whether or not they need a lot of suns, a lot of water, or a plethora of shade. The vibes that you feel when you are around plants in their natural atmosphere will easily change over to them when you bring them into your home.

Once you have experienced herbs in their natural habitat, it's time to bring them to your home. You can buy seeds or pre-started plants at a variety of different locations. It is important to note that starting your plants from seeds is the best way to grow as that means you'll be cultivating them from the moment they start to sprout. You can add good intentions and positive energy to them from the moment they are planted.

One of the people's biggest concerns about growing their herbs at home is the fact that they don't have much room. This can seem to be a bit difficult, especially if you live in a small apartment.

However, there are a variety of different ways that you can still grow herbs at your home regardless of where you live.

If you reside in a small space, one option is to plant your herbs in pots. There are a large number of different sized pots that can easily be rested on shelves near windows or in windowsills. Pots don't take up a large amount of room, which will make it easy to fit them into your small space. Having a potted plant garden in your home will provide you with comfort, as well as the critical herbs that you need for a variety of different Wiccan practices.

One other option is to purchase some window boxes. When you are in a small space, you can hang window boxes outside of each window so that you will have plenty of room for planting. You need to be slightly careful with this as some herbs won't want a ton of sunlight while others will. So, location is going to matter to ensure that they are getting the proper amount of sunlight throughout the day.

Obviously, if you have more space building a garden will be a bit easier. Plants do best when they are outside. So, if you have an outside space that you can build a garden in, it will be the most advantageous. Some people like to do raised gardens as they look very nice for landscaping purposes. Others like to build a traditional garden. Either way, it is completely fine as long as you provide a plethora of love and attention to the herbs that you are trying to grow.

Once you have grown herbs, you will then need to harvest them. It is important to note that you can purchase already dried herbs from a variety of different stores. Here again, growing your own and drying them yourself is going to provide you with herbs that hold more power than ones that you would buy at a store. In addition, herbs that you buy from a grocery store tend to go bad very quickly, so you'll need to use them fast. When you drive them at home, you typically get a better shelf life out of them.

Most of the time, you will gather your herbs in bunches. You will simply need to tie a string around the bottom of the bunch and hang it upside down to dry. There are other ways of drying herbs; however, this is going to be your safest bet. It is advantageous to look up your herbs individually to know exactly how they need to be dried, but this is the manner in which you will do it more often than not.

After your herbs have dried, you will need to store them. There are a variety of different ways that you can store your herbs. At the end of the day, you simply need to make sure that they are in an airtight container. Many people prefer to use glass jars for herb storage. Glass jars are probably your best bet, and you will get the most longevity out of your dried herbs with them.

If you are unable to create any sort of garden at home, you do have the option of gathering them from the wild. We discussed this briefly before. When you are gathering herbs from the wild, you need to be very careful and have a great base of knowledge surrounding herbs. Many plants look similar, and this could end up being dangerous. You may think that you are getting one thing but end up with a plant that is actually poisonous. Obviously, this is something that needs to be avoided.

If you decide to collect your herbs from the wild, it is advantageous to invest in a book that will help you identify them. Books can provide you with the small intricacies that make finding the correct herb easier. In addition to learning about the herbs that you are looking for, you should become familiar with the herbs that grow in your region. Many herbs only grow in a particular area of the world. This will mean that if you need to fill in the gaps, you would need to purchase your herbs from a store or a nursery.

Chapter 3: Charging Herbs, Herbal Bathing, & Herbal Teas

In this chapter, you gain valuable knowledge on how to add positive energy to your herbs so that you can use them in spellcasting. By charging your herbs, you will have higher success rates when manifesting spells. It does not take a plethora of time, but it is an important step in the process.

After looking at charging, we are going to discuss herbal bathing. There are a variety of different spells and positive outcomes that happen when you take baths that you have added herbs too. Not only will we look at herbal bathing, but we will also give you a couple of spells that can be used during these baths.

Lastly, we will take a look at herbal teas. Tea is fantastic for divination spells. You can also use them for spells for energy, luck, and prosperity. It is amazing the effects a cup of herbal tea can have on your mind, body, and spirit.

Charging Herbs

Charging your herbs is an important process to ensure that they are going to hold a lot of power for spellcasting. When you first plant your seeds or starter plants, you need to charge them. If you do not charge them at this time, you will need to charge them before using them for magical purposes. Some like to charge them at both steps to ensure that they have the highest level of energy possible. This should be done with your own magical energy. Charging your herbs is not a complicated or lengthy process; however, it is a critical one.

One of the best ways to charge your herbs is to take them outside and sit down on the ground. You should then clear your mind and sent her yourself. Spending some time grounding your root chakra is also advantageous. This will allow you to connect with the Earth's energy below you. Start a simple meditation that is focused on bringing the positive earth energy into your body. You should do this while holding the herb plants or seeds in your hands.

As you focus on the energy moving into your body, you should then see it inside of yourself, moving to the herbs you are holding. Some people like to use mantras to help ensure that their energy is combined with the plants or seeds energy.

Another time that you need to make sure to charge your herbs is if you are using herbs that have been dried and sitting for a while. As an herb sets after being dried, it loses some of its energy, and that energy will need to be replaced. Fresh herbs that have just been dried tend to have higher levels of NRG, so if you charged them before planting them, likely, you wouldn't have to worry about this step when you go to use them for spellcasting.

The process to recharge already dried herbs is the same. It is all about intent, focus, and meditation. You can also enhance the positive energy flow by using tools like crystals and candles. Later on, in this book, we will discuss candles and crystals, which will provide you with more information as to how they can help you when casting herbal spells.

Herbal Bathing

Herbal bathing is also frequently called ritual bathing. It is important as it can enhance your magical energy and provide you with the right state of mind to perform a variety of magical practices. It helps to remove negative energy from your mind, body, and soul. Herbal bathing is a practice that has been done for generations and will continue to be a predominant aspect of herbal magic.

More often than not, herbal bathing is used for purification. It can help calm and relax you. Additionally, the healing properties of herbal bathing are amazing. The aromas are extremely therapeutic and affect people on a spiritual level like few other things. It can also help you find balance.

The benefits of herbal bathing are plentiful. On a physical level, it can help you improve circulation, handle sleep issues, and promote healthy skin. Mentally, it can provide you with stress relief and a reduction of anxiety. You will feel more relaxed, calm, and warm after participating in herbal bathing. It will also provide you with a better connection and awareness to the more spiritual side of things.

Creating an herbal bath is not difficult. For the most part, you can simply add a variety of different herbs into your bathtub. Other times, you will need to boil water and add the herbs in so that you can extract their oils and energy. This is not always required; it simply depends on what you are trying to achieve.

If you are looking for protection or purification, there is a very simple bath that you can create. You will need to steep basil in 1 cup of boiling water. After it has steeped, you should remove the herb from the water. From there, you will simply add it to your bathwater. Once you enter into the bathtub, you will need to relax and meditate with the specific intent of being protected or purified. After you have finished this bathing ritual, you should let your body air dry. By removing the moisture with a towel that can inhibit the effectiveness of this bathing ritual.

Another great spell that can be accomplished with herbal bathing will help to cleanse the negative energies that have attached themselves to you. To accomplish this, you will need to start by casting a circle in your bathroom. You should call the elements and light a couple of candles that are lavender in color.

This spell is a bit trickier as you will need to create a sachet. A sachet is simply a bag that contains different items. For this one, you will need chamomile, lavender, and Rosemary that has been dried and crushed. From there, you will simply hang it over your faucet and run your bath. The water will flow over the sachet and infuse your bath with the properties of these magical herbs. Once the bath has been drawn, you should add roughly 1/2 of a cup of lemon juice.

Submerge yourself in the bathwater and relax. You should focus on your breathing. With your eyes closed, visualize that the stress, tension, and negative energy is leaving your body. Put yourself into a meditative state and continue to focus on the release of negativity. You should stay in this meditative state for several minutes.

Once you feel relaxed and clean of the negativities that have been burdening you, you can remove yourself from the bathtub. Here again, you should allow your body to dry naturally instead of toweling off. This will make the spell more effective. It is important to note that you will need to clean your bathtub thoroughly to ensure that there is no residue left behind. This will also ensure that the negative energy is washed away from your life completely.

If you find that your life has been in a state of chaos lately, taking an herbal bath for peace may be advantageous. There are a variety of different bathing practices that can bring peace to your surroundings, and we're going to provide you with one of our favorites. There are more steps to this bath than with others, so take your time and focus on what you were doing throughout each step.

First, you should run your bath and pour about a tablespoon of milk into it. You should then add 6 to 8 rose petals. It does not matter if they're fresh or if they have been dried. Move the Rose petals and milk around your bathtub with your fingers.

Once you have added these ingredients and while you are still mixing them around, you should say something like "Water ripples in the wind, pollen moves through the air, more silent than a peaceful sea, a burning desire to bring peacefulness here." This will help power the peacefulness you are searching for in your life.

After chanting this mantra for a few moments, you can step into the magical herbal bath you have created. Lighting some white candles can also help improve the level of power this spell will hold. Meditate while in the bath on the fact that you no longer want chaos in your life. Focus your intent on peace. Allow the water to take the negative energies away from you and allow the peacefulness of the herb mixture to replace it.

Once you have meditated on peacefulness in your life for several minutes, you can step out of the bathtub. As with other ritual baths, you should allow yourself to air dry. Drain and clean the tub to remove the chaos that has been consuming your life. Gather the rose petals and bury them far away from your house. From here, you are sure to notice a new sense of calm surround you and your home.

While there is a plethora of different herbal baths that can be used for magical practices, we're only going to look at one more. This is a bath that can help fill your life with love. Love spells are some of the most common and also some of the most dangerous. You need to be careful when entertaining the idea of casting love spells. This is a bit safer due to the fact that it is simply going to help open you up to the prospect of love. You will not be casting an actual love spell on another human being.

To create a bath that can make you more desirable, you should fill your bathtub with warm water. It is important that it is not extremely hot. From there, you will add 4 to 5 navel oranges. Additionally, you should add a bunch of mint leaves that are fresh. You will then get into the bathtub.

After you are in the tub, you should remove the peels of the oranges and squeeze the orange juice into the water. You should rub the peels and the fruit on to your skin, as well as your hair. After this, you should do the same with the mint leaves. Many people like to chew on a mint leaf to enhance the power of this spell.

Once you have completed these steps, you need to enter into a calm state of meditation. As with all spells, your intent needs to be set and clear. For this value need to focus on the fact that you want to become more desirable to the people that are meant to bring love into your life. Focus and meditate on this aspect for as long as possible. This process should be repeated several days in a row.

After you have meditated on this for several minutes, you can remove yourself from the bathtub. Allow your body to air dry rather than drying yourself with a towel. You do not need to hold on to any of the fruit or herbs that you have placed in the bathtub; you can simply throw them away. As you continue to use this herbal bath, you will find that people are finding you to be more irresistible than ever before.

Herbal Teas

Now that we have discussed the amazing potential of herbal bathing, we're going to move on to herbal teas. Herbal teas have been used for a variety of different practices throughout the centuries. Additionally, you can find herbal teas used in just about every culture found around the world. Sure, teas can be delicious and soothing to us to drink, but they also hold a large variety of magical powers. You can accomplish things like divination, extra luck in life, and prosperity through the use of herbal teas.

Magic with tease is extremely powerful. It can cast spells, as well as allow us the ability of divination. When which is practice with tea magic, they tend to be calm and powerful. The herbs they use provide them with the ability to center themselves easily and gain insight and enlightenment about the world we can see and the world we cannot.

Tea is not only used for drinking. Many and people also use it to build sachets or stuff their pillows. It can lead to a great night's sleep, as well as allowing you to create a variety of different charms. Negative thoughts and energies can easily be removed when using tea magic.

Most types of herbal teas come from the same leaves; However, there are absolutely different varieties of tea. Also, different parts of the plants are used to bring even more variety. Certain teas will have better or more powerful magical properties based on your intended use.

There are a few different plans that tea is made from an herbalist will easily recognize the difference. Some are grown on tops of mountains while others can be grown near large bodies of water. Depending on the outcome you are looking for will determine the type of tea you want to use. The time of year also plays a role in which tea you should choose for your magical purpose.

Black tea is known for being good at providing the user with courage. In addition, it can be excellent when you are feeling bored, as it will bring excitement to your life. This type of tea is most used for creating spells to bring money into your life. It can also stimulate your mind so that you are more conscious of the world around you.

If you need to bring money into your life using black tea, magic can be very helpful. One spell you can use is quite simple. You will hold the teabag between both hands before you use it in your glass of hot water. While holding it, you should visualize that money is coming into your life. See yourself obtaining rich is and how you will use them. Focus on being happy and wealthy. After you have pushed your intent into your black tea, you will steep it in your water while continuing to focus on the outcome you wish to manifest. From there, drink your tea as normal. Doing this for several days in a row will help ensure that money will come your way.

Oolong tea also provides a variety of different magical properties. It is known to help bring serenity and love into a person's life. It can also help you reflect on your past to help bring emotional balance to your future. This type of tea is also fantastic if you are working on divination practices or trying to foretell the future.

Many people use oolong tea for love spells. Here again, you will hold the teabag between both of your hands, and you will need to meditate and visualize that love is coming into your life. Take the time to truly see what your ideal partner looks like and acts like. The more details you can think of, the better. This includes visualizing what it will feel like when they touch you and how you will react when you are near them. You need true and intense focus during this procedure. The meditation process should last longer than normal. Once you have pushed your intent into the tea bag, you can steep it in your hot water and drink it. You must continue to perform this tea spell to ensure that love comes into your life.

Divination through tea leaves is extremely common. It is one of the best tools you can do when working on your divination skills. The practice of reading tea leaves is an ancient practice that will continue on for generations to come. When you read tea leaves, you are interpreting symbols that the leaves configure themselves in. While this type of divination may not be as popular as crystal reading or tarot, it is still commonly used. Divination through tea leaves is not as popular because there is a lot of room for error. It is not a completely understood act, and the way we see a pattern may be quite different than how someone else does. When we see things differently, naturally, we are going to read them differently.

When you are trying to accomplish divination through reading the leaves of tea, it really is all about focusing your energy. All magic comes from your intent. You should press your intention into the tea, and this will allow them to show you the signs of whatever question you are searching for answers for. It can show you glimpses of the past, present, or future. There are a variety of different texts available that can help you understand what the symbol of your tea leaves is trying to show you.

When you are working on divination through reading your tea leaves, there is a process that must be followed. First, you must make a cup of tea. Your teacup should be light in color. Additionally, you need to use loose tea leaves, not ones that are contained inside of a bag. It is important to note that simply opening a bag of tea will not work. The leaves that they use are much too fine to be able to form into obvious patterns.

After making your cup of tea, you should take some time and focus on your intentions. Doing this while holding the cup is most advantageous. It allows your energy to transfer into the tea leaves housed inside of your cup. Regardless of who is seeking answers, the intent from the person doing the divination is what is most important. The question that you ask should be concise.

Once the water has cooled to a drink bull temperature, you should start sipping the tea. As you drink it, you need to visualize and focus on the question at hand continuously. You should drink all but about a tablespoon of the tea. The leaves will settle at the bottom. From here, you will hold the cup and swirl it three times in a clockwise direction.

After swirling it three times, you should flip the cup over onto a saucer. It should remain in this position for roughly a minute. You will then again rotate it three times. From here, flip the cup back over into an upright position. The tea leaves should be stuck to the cup, creating different shapes. This is where it is time to look into them and read the story of what they have to say.

You will need to put some time and research into what different symbols look like and mean to be able to accomplish divination through reading tea leaves properly. It can be a lot of work; however, the results are absolutely amazing. Whether you are working on divination for yourself or the people around you, it can provide you with true insight into what is to come. As with all things, practice makes perfect. So, don't get discouraged. Just continue to practice, and reading your leaves will become simpler as time goes on.

Chapter 4: Sachets & Essential Oils

Chapter four is going to cover such cool magical practices. We will start with a discussion on magical sachets. Sachets are a versatile item that can help you in a variety of ways. We will explain their importance and how you can go about creating a variety of different sachets and the uses for each one.

There will also be information on essential oils. Sure, you can buy essential oils just about anywhere, but you are likely getting an infusion, not an actual essential oil. There are ways to create your own at home. We will go over the process of how to make your own essential oils and the uses that they serve in your magical practices.

Sachets

Sachets are also known as charm bags. These are an easy way to create and cast a spell while housing it in a simple bag. There are a variety of different items that can go into a sachet. It all depends on the spell that you are trying to cast. It can include things like herbs, essential oils, stones, crystals, or amulets.

These bags are extremely simple to make. They are typically made from a square of fabric that you tie together. Sometimes, people will use an embroidered cloth or draw markings of their intent on the outside of the sachet. It can be made of a variety of different materials. The most common is to make them out of burlap or cotton; However, people have also been known to make them out of leather, silk, or a variety of other fabrics. Honestly, the fabric that you use is not as important as the spell that you put inside of it.

The color of your sachet bag also plays a role in the success of your spell. Let's take a moment and look at what different colored bags will help you with in terms of the spell you are trying to cast. Obviously, we cannot go over every color on the spectrum, but we will cover some of the most popular ones.

A gold-colored sachet will help to empower spells that are used to bring wealth into your life. They are also good when you are looking for protection for yourself or for your home. If you are trying to connect with the higher powers of the universe, a gold-colored sachet will also work well.

Using a silver piece of cloth will help increase a spell that is used for prosperity. Silver is also fantastic when you are performing moon magic. If you are trying to enhance your psychic abilities or get into contact with the female higher powers, silver will do the trick.

When you are trying to build a sachet for healing, you will want to use a yellow piece of cloth. This color is also good if you are struggling to find employment, or you need to find added resources in your life. While not as common, a yellow cloth can also be used when you are trying to bring warmth and happiness into your home.

Next, we move on to orange. Using an orange covering can promote spells for communication. It is important to note that orange is also the color related to your throat chakra, which is the center of your ability to communicate with yourself, as well as others. An orange sachet can make relaying messages easier and clearer. It can also help promote things like travel between realms and astral projection.

Green is a very popular color for sachets. It covers a wide variety of different wants and needs. If you are searching for prosperity, you will want to use a green sachet covering. It is also fantastic when you are trying to nurture the growth of friendships and relationships. Green sachets can put you in a better connection with the abundant energy that nature has to offer us.

Creating a charm that will bring justice to a difficult situation will require cloth made from purple. Purple sachets are also good when you are trying to find higher levels of wisdom or solve the mysteries of your life. It can also help bring wealth to you when you are going through times of financial struggle.

Sachets that are made with a red cloth will heighten the romance that is in your life. Red cloth is also fantastic if you are searching for strength. With that strength, you will also be able to find success in your daily life. Many protection spells are housed within red sachets, as well.

If you find that you are struggling with friendships, using a pink cloth for your sachet is advantageous. The pink fabric is also going to help open your heart to love and allow love to find you. Not only that, there is a variety of different healing spells that are more easily manifested when using pink as the outer covering of the sachet.

Last, but not least, there is the black sashay. A black outer covering is fantastic for removing negative energies from your life. It can absorb any hexes that may be cast on you. It also helps to alleviate stress and anxiety due to nefarious intentions that other people are placing on you.

Here again, this is only a look at the many colors that you could use when building a magical sachet. More often than not, one of these colors is going to work just fine. Keep in mind that most of the bags will close with a drawstring closure, which will allow you to open them and add materials if you need too. On occasion, you will completely, so a sachet shut; however, that is not typically the case.

When you are creating a sachet, you should also consider this shape. If you are working on a love spell, it is obviously going to be advantageous to shape it as a heart. This is not the most important piece, but it can add a bit of power to your sachet and ensure that the spell you are trying to cast is able to manifest completely.

Now that you have a basic understanding as to what a sachet is, let's move on. From here, we're going to give you some ideas on different sachets you can create. We will look at sachets that can be used for luck, protection, love, and health.

When you are creating a sachet for a luck spell, you will want to use a bag that is colored in either gold, green, or silver. They will all work quite well to help you reach your intended purpose. The items that go inside once you create the bag may vary, but some good things to go after are:

- **Herbs:**
    - Clover
    - Nutmeg
    - Fenugreek
    - Ginger

- **Stones:**
    - Green Agate
    - Tiger's Eye
    - Sunstone

- **Extras:**

  - Spanish Moss

  - Irish Moss

  - Small Horseshoe (You can also draw or paint a horseshoe on the outside material of the sachet)

Once you have put this sachet together, you will need to push your intent into it. This is most easily done while in a meditative state. Focus your thoughts an visualize what your life will look like when your luck has improved. Many people also like to add a mantra to this type of luck spell. You can go with something like, "Fortune and luck find me this day; for all I seek is coming my way."

Protection is a common need, and sashays are fantastic for helping us gain it. This can be protected from a variety of different things. It can help keep the negative energies that are surrounding us at bay. Additionally, those that have malicious intent toward us can be thwarted in their practices by using a magical sachet. To create a protection sachet, you will need a bag that is black, red, or gold in color. It should be filled with:

- **Herbs:**

  - Cedar

- o Mint

- o Cinnamon

- o Betony

- **Gems:**

  - o Amber

  - o Black Tourmaline

  - o Malachite

- **Extras:**

  - o A Sea Shell

  - o A Piece of a Straw Broom

Intent and meditation always play a role after creating a sachet. During the creation process, you should keep your mind focused on why you are creating it. After it has been created, spending time to meditate over it and push the correct energy into it will always be advantageous and ensure that the manifestation of your outcome works appropriately. Finding a mantra or a prayer to use when creating these sachets is always a good plan, as well. One that will work well with this protection sachet is, "Energies that are dark must rid my space, and in that the light will replace."

Love sachets are also a very common desire for many people. They will not only help to bring love into your life; they will also allow you to accept love if you are afraid of it. Love sachets are a mild way to bring love into your life. They are not nearly as risky as many other love spells that you may have looked at in the past. You need to be careful when you are playing with matters of the heart. To create a love spell sachet, you'll want to use a bag that is pink or red in color. It should contain:

- **Herbs:**

    o   Rose Petals

    o   Cinnamon Sticks

    o   Lavender

- **Gems:**

    o   Pink Kunzite

    o   Rose Quartz

- **Extras:**

    o   Maple   Leaves

While you are meditating impressing your intent into this sachet, you need to focus on the type of love that you are trying to bring into your life. If intimate love is what you are looking for, you should focus on the attributes of your ideal partner. If it is a friendship that you are searching for you should think about the things that are the most important to you in terms of someone being a good friend. during your meditations, you should use a prayer or a mantra similar to this: "With the four elements earth, air, fire, and water, please let the powers at be bring love forward and on to me."

Last but not least, we are going to teach you how to create a sachet that will help improve your health. This is not only your physical health but also your mental and spiritual health. When you are looking for healing of any variety, a sachet made with material that is blue or yellow. You should fill your blue or yellow sachet with:

- **Herbs:**
    - Thyme
    - St. John's Wort
    - Peppermint
- **Gems:**
    - Sunstone
    - Amethyst
    - Toadstone

- **Extras:**

  - Symbol   of   the   Sun

Your meditation should be focused on healing. You should visualize yourself being mentally, spiritually, and physically strong. See yourself overcoming great mental and physical feats. You should also, as always, focus your intent on the sachet as you hold it in your hands. The mantra, "Healing my mind, body, and spirit, so it is fit and strong will strengthen my heart and allow my body to carry on," is a pretty good one for accomplishing the task of making an effective healing sachet.

Once you have created a sachet for your intended purpose, you can either carry it around on your person or sleep with it near you. The more often you have it near you, the more effective it is going to be. It can be carried in a pocket, purse, or Simply put in a place that you are frequently in. Sachets cold very powerful magic and the energy inside of them can be enhanced by continually meditating with them.

Essential Oils

Essential oils have played a vital role in rituals and the magical practice of Wiccans for an extreme amount of time. The traditional use of essential oils in magical practices help to bring the positive energies of nature into your life. Additionally, it can help manifest the change that you have been searching for.

Scented oils have been used by priests, healers, and shamans throughout all of the recorded histories on magical rituals and medicine. They are combined with incense, tinctures, appointments, and charms to be used for just about anything you can imagine.

A variety of different sources can be used in making essential oils. This can include all pieces of a plant. It does take some hard work and dedication to create your own essential oils, but you won't receive the best outcomes from ones that come to fruition through your own hands. You can purchase essential oils from a variety of different places; however, they're not always genuine essential oils. Frequently they are simple infusions of an herb or a plant with a different oil. They are not the actual oils that come from a plant itself. This is one of the main reasons that creating your own essential oils is advantageous.

While essential oils can play a major role in casting spells, they are typically not the main feature. They are used to anoint a variety of different ritualistic tools. This includes things like crystals, talismans, and amulets. Candle magic is also heightened with the use of essential oils. Realistically, if you want to add energy and enhance your spells, the use of essential oils is going to give you the power that you are searching for.

If you try and purchase actual essential oils, it can be quite expensive. Creating them on your own can absolutely save you some money. It may take a bit of time to compile a good collection of these magical oils, but it will be well worth it. You need to be careful if you are buying your essential oils to make sure that they are pure oils from plants. Oftentimes, people will use an oil base and combine them with plant materials. This is an infusion, not a true essential oil.

Infusions are not the only problem. Unfortunately, there are a lot of manmade processed products that are labeled as essential oils. These do not actually contain any plant-based materials but are made with random oils and sense. These would do you no good if you were trying to use them with spellcasting. Due to this fact, many witches prefer to create their own essential oils even though it is a bit of a process.

One method that is pretty simple that you can use to make your own essential oils will simply require a crockpot. You will take your crockpot and fill it about halfway with the plant of your choosing. Stripping the leaves off of the stems and cutting the stems into small pieces will be advantageous. Many people also like to rip the leaves as it makes the oils come out a bit easier.

Once you have filled your crockpot about halfway with your plant, you will then add water. The water should come about an inch above your plant material. You should still have a decent amount of room at the Top of your crockpot. Instead of putting the lid on in the normal fashion, you will actually put it on upside down. This will allow the steam to fall back inside of the crockpot more easily.

Once you have this setup, you will turn your crockpot on high. You should allow it to stay on high for roughly one to two hours. Then you will be able to turn the crockpot down to low. Once it is in its lowest setting, you should allow it to cook for roughly four more hours.

After the four hours have passed, turn the crockpot off and let the mixture cool completely. Once it has completely cooled, you should place the entire crockpot in your refrigerator. Allow it to sit overnight. It is extremely important that you follow this step carefully. If your crockpot is too hot when you put it in the refrigerator, it could crack or damage it.

The following day, you'll be able to remove your mixture from the refrigerator. What you were going to notice is that there is now an oily white residue floating on the top of the water. It should be quite hard. You will need to remove this oil carefully and quickly.

If you do not do it quickly, it will start to melt in your hands. The essential oils that you are gathering can be placed into any sort of bottle. The bottle should have a lid and glasses, typically what people go after as they like to use dropper bottles. Make sure that you put a label on the container so you know what each bottle is housing.

As you can see, it will take a bit of time to make essential oils. However, it is not that difficult. This is why most people prefer to make their own. Additionally, you can energize and push your intent into each one of the oils as you create them. Storing them in a dark-colored glass container will keep them from spoiling and allow them to hold on to their energy longer.

When you first start creating essential oils, it is best to do single oils. However, Azure collection grows you can also make blends. The process is exactly the same except for the fact that you will use two different types of plant matter instead of just one. After collecting a blended mix of essential oils, you should give it some time before using it. This will allow it the time it needs for their energies to truly merge.

We have only provided you with one way to create your own essential oils. It is one of the easiest ways to do it at home. Basically, everyone has a crockpot lying around, so it is going to be simple, and it won't require a major investment. However, keep in mind that there are absolutely other ways to create your own essential oils. There are many books in articles related to the topic, and it would only take a bit of research to find another way if you don't find this one particularly interesting. Keep in mind that this really is one of the easiest methods, and it will ensure that you are getting pure essential oils.

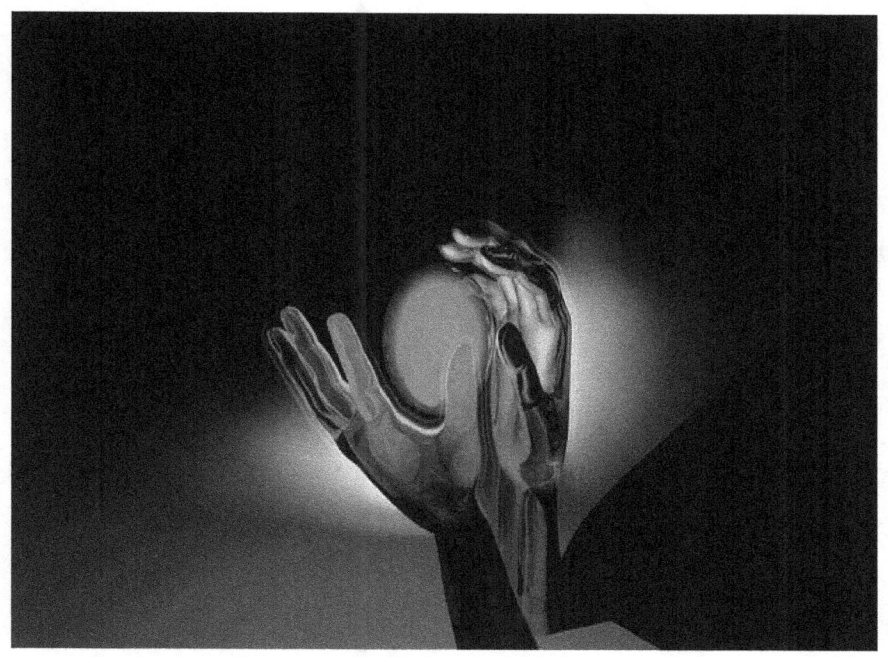

Chapter 5: Basic Herbs & Beginner Spells

In chapter 2, we provided you with ten basic herbs that every person should have at their disposal. Obviously, there are many other herbs that are going to work well with your magical practices. In this chapter, we are going to take a look at the best herbs to use for your magical practices. Some of the ten herbs we talked about earlier will be included, but we have also included a few others that are great basic herbs to start working with.

Additionally, this chapter will provide you with spells for each herb that we discussed. These will be for beginners. Each spell will be quite easily accomplished. There will be spells that can help you with success, money, luck, prosperity, love, anxiety, pain, and reproductive health. There really is a spell out there for everyone to help with just about every situation. This is especially true with herbal spells.

The first herb that we want to talk about is sage. Sage has a variety of different magical properties that can be truly helpful to you and your life. It is known for being great in purification and healing spells. It is also advantageous to use it when you are trying to cleanse ritual tools or banish evil from your life. Sage is also fantastic when you are looking for wisdom or a better understanding of a difficult situation. It can help ease pain and allow you to take in the lessons that life has to teach us.

One of the most common spells that are performed with a sage bundle is used to cleanse an area of evil spirits. If your home is being haunted or you feel as if someone has cast a hex earn you burning sage can be a great way to handle it. Performing this spell is exceptionally easy. All you will need is a bundle of sage and a strong intent. If there is a certain area of your home that seems to have more negativity than others, that is where you should start. Move around to all the corners of the room and waft the sage smoke around it. While you do this, you should be focused on the intent of banishing the nefarious energies that are surrounding you and your life. It is especially important to pay attention to the doorways between rooms.

Bay Laurel is another herb that has a variety of magical purposes. It can provide a user with visions of prophecy. It can also provide clarity to their life. Many have been known to use Bay Laurel in spells for cleansing and purification. It can help bring success and positive energy into a person's life. On top of all of these attributes, and is also good for making wishes come true and bringing love into your life.

If you were trying to cast a spell for prophetic dreams, Bay Laurel is going to help you with this. Whatever question you are trying to answer should be written down on a plain sheet of white paper without lines on it. Once you have written your question down, you should brew a cup of Bay Laurel tea. Take the tea and your question to your bedroom. Please the paper on the floor next to your bed. After setting it there, drink the tea that you just brewed and concentrate on the conundrum at hand. When you fall, asleep your question should be answered. After your question has been answered, you should burn the piece of paper that you wrote it down on. This shows honor to the prophetic spirits that helped guide you on your journey toward understanding.

Rosemary also holds a large variety of magical properties. If you are looking to cast a spell for beauty, rejuvenation, or love, it has a variety of attributes that will aid you in them. It is also known to be good for protection and purification spells. If you are searching for empowerment or clarity in a difficult situation, Rosemary is a great herb to cast a spell with. A great tip when it comes to Rosemary is to burn a few of its leaves before casting any spells. It will allow you to relax and purify your surroundings prior to spellcasting. Additionally, you will find that you are free of nightmares after burning a few of these leaves. Rosemary is great for ensuring you have positive dreams.

Next, let's talk about basil. Basil has magical properties that can help bring luck and money into your life. Additionally, it can be used in a variety of different love spells. Spells that use basil will help to bring blessings in abundance into a person's life. It has also been found that spells using basil can help with clarity, protection, and purification.

If your finances have been less than stellar lately, basil can help bring money into your life. This spell is one of the absolute easiest spells to create. As with all things, your intention is key. To cast a spell with Basil to bring money into your life, you will simply need a basil leaf. You should draw a symbol for money on the leaf. Once you have drawn the symbol on it, you should hold the leaf between the two of your hands. Find a relaxing place and meditate with the leaf loosely held in your hands. Obviously, you need to focus your intention on what your life will be like and what it will look like once money comes to you. After ending your meditation session, you simply need to place the leaf inside of your wallet. Meditating on this leaf several days in a row will help enhance the power of your spell.

Lavender is another basic herb that everyone should have on hand. It is commonly used in spells that bring love, beauty, luck, and attraction into one's life. It is also fantastic if someone has malintent toward or you need to protect yourself from negativity. It can be powerful when you need to banish nefarious entities from your life and provide protection to yourself or your home.

Finding love is something that many people seek. Lavender can absolutely help you in this venture. Women will have more success using this love spell to gain a man than men well with women. Too cast a love spell using lavender, you will need to create a sachet. A good example of one to make is listed in the chapter that discusses is sachets. Once the sachet is created, you will need to meditate your intentions of love into it. Focus on your idea of the perfect mate. Envision what it would be like to be around them and how you would both feel after being in each other's company. After completing your meditation, you should place the sachet under your pillow. Sleep with it here for seven nights. The same meditation should be completed each night before placing it under your pillow. After you have completed this, you will find that love enters your life quite quickly.

If you want to add some extra power to this spell, it is quite possible. Lavender can be found in essential oils, soaps, and incense. If you're going to be using lavender essential oils, it is best to make your own. Using all three of these products, you can add an amazing amount of power to the love spell that has been cast. A few dabs of lavender essential oil on your sachet and also on your wrists will enhance the power. Washing your body with lavender-scented soap and burning lavender-scented incense throughout your home will also help to empower this spell.

Next, we will talk about vanilla. Vanilla is fantastic if you are trying to improve your sensuality. It is also good for spells of seduction and love. Vanilla is known for being used in spells for peace, luck, and enhancing business. You can also use it when you are trying to achieve prophetic or lucid dreams. There really are a lot of magical uses for vanilla.

Once in a while, we all experience a point in our life where we are feeling a bit down. If you are looking for a good spell to make your home and your life happy, one is utilizing vanilla, maybe the answer. To create this spell, you will need to make a mixture of vanilla that has been powdered and sugar. It should be stored in a glass jar that seals tightly. By simply putting this jar in a window of your home happiness and peace will be attracted to you. You will also find that the level of affection you experience is amplified. You can use this mixture as a body scrub to enhance the effects of this happiness spell.

Another great spell that you can cast quite easily using vanilla will help to improve your business. The financial gain in business is critically important. If you are finding that you are lacking the income that you need to sustain your life, a spell with vanilla will help you find the extra income that you need. To cast this spell, you will need to use a fluffy piece of cotton. Soak the cotton in vanilla oil and a few drops of Wintergreen essential oil. From there, sprinkle a teaspoon of cinnamon over the top of the cotton. Put the cotton near the area that you store money in your business. Spend some time meditating your intent to not only the piece of cotton but also the area in which you keep the money. Once you have placed your intent, you will find that money quickly starts pouring into your business.

Patchouli is another plant that has a variety of magical attributes. It has been used for spells that can help bring prosperity and money into one's life. Patchouli is also good when you are looking for lust or for true love. Many people commonly use this herb when they are casting spells for fertility. There is a large variety of spells that can be cast using this herb, and these are only a small look at them. It really is an essential herbed have around.

This herb is fantastic when you are performing an herbal bath spell for fertility. To do this, you will need to put a pink candle in a green candle near your bathtub. You should also have a Seven-day candle that is scented with natural patchouli. From there, you will run a bath and add about ten drops of patchouli essential oil. Then add a few drops of lemon essential oil, orange essential oil, and lime essential oil to the bathwater. Light the candles and stand in the bathtub as you do this focus on your intent. Scoop some of the water into a container and pour it over your head. Continue to pour water over your body until you are completely soaked.

Sit down in the bathtub and relax. From here, you will want to get into the deepest level of meditation that you can. Envision what your pregnancy will be like. You should also focus on how you are going to feel when a baby is brought into the world. Focusing on the candle flames can help you reach the state of relaxation that you will need to achieve this level of meditation. You need to hold the meditation for 15 to 20 minutes. After doing so, remove yourself from the bathtub and allow your body to air dry. Repeat this spell for seven days, and you will be well on your way to becoming pregnant.

Now we're going to talk about Apple blossoms. There is an amazing amount of different magical properties that are associated with Apple blossoms. More often than not, people use these wonderful smelling flowers when working on love spells. They are also fantastic for healing rituals. Many people believe that if you are trying to connect with the goddess is these blossoms can help you achieve it. They are quite spiritual in nature, which is why they will provide you with a great connection with the higher powers, as well as the universe.

Love spells that are performed with Apple blossoms are extremely common. Let's take a look at one that can help bring love or romance back into your life after it has been lacking. You will want to start by surrounding yourself in pink and red candles. They should form a circle. You will sit cross-legged in the middle. Light the candles and hold a branch with Apple blossoms between your two hands. As you focus your intent, remove the petals from the flower. Sprinkle the Flowers around you in a clockwise motion. While you are doing this, you need to continue to focus and push your intent out into the world. Using a mantra like, "Apple blossoms filled with love rain your power down on me from above." Allow your candles to burn all the way down and leave the flower petals in a circle until they start to wilt. Once they wilt, remove them, and bury them somewhere near your home.

After doing so, you will find new love or a new spark occurring in your current relationship.

Chamomile is another great herb for spellcasting rituals. Simply drinking it is known to help calm anxiety and bring peaceful sleep. Many also use it to bring money into their lives. It has been known to be used to combat hexes that have been cast upon you. When you drink this tea prior to performing a ritual, it can help you focus your energy and heighten it. Prosperity spells, as well as healing spells, frequently include this herb. You may also find it to be helpful when you use it during dreamwork or trying to remove negative energy from your life. It is frequently combined with other herbs to enhance its magical properties.

If your life is strewn with negative energies or you have bad feelings around your home, chamomile is great for dealing with it. You will simply start by brewing an extremely strong cup of chamomile tea. You should then stir a tablespoon of honey into it in a counterclockwise direction. While doing this, you will want to say something like, "Negative energy get out of my way, allow me peace, and all bad feelings go away." From here, you will walk around your house and allow the steam from your hot cup of tea to move around the room. Continue to recite a line like the one from above and focus your intent on removing the negativity from your life or your home.

Mugwort is an extremely versatile herb that almost every witch is going to have available to them at a moment's notice. It is frequently used to Ward off psychic attacks and keep a high level of protection. Many have found that it is also good when you are working on healing. More often than not, this herb is used to help bring about prophetic dreams. It can also be used in incense for divination. It is important to note that there are a variety of different experiences that are associated with this herb and you need to be careful when working with it.

There are some warnings that you must consider before using this herb. It is not safe for pregnant women to use. It does contain toxins that could build up in the liver if you use it excessively. You should never ingest this herb. Many people are allergic to the pollen that comes off of this plant. Additionally, it has been noted that skin irritation may occur if you come into direct contact with it.

Mugwort is fantastic to use when you are trying to open your psychic channels or if you are working on scrying. To do this, you need to infuse incense with Mugwort essential oil. Once this has been accomplished, burn the incense, and let the smoke and scent fill the room. From here, it is all about intent and meditation. Focus on your desired outcome as the smoke fills the room. The magical properties, scent, and smoke will help put you in the right frame of mind and energize your magical workings.

Last but not least, we are going to discuss the herb Yarrow. It is awesome when you are looking for a protective shield. Additionally, it can help you delve into the spiritual world much more easily. It is commonly used for divination as well as psychic awareness. You will find that when you work with this herb, you can see things more clearly, and your magical experiences are heightened. Yarrow is also good when you are working on healing spells.

A great use for Yarrow in your magical practices is to use it to bring about prophetic dreams. To accomplish this, you will need to create a dream pillow stuffed with the Flowers of the Yarrow plant. You should write your question on a plain white piece of paper and add it to the dream pillow you have created. You will then need to focus your intent. As with all things, this can be done during a deep state of meditation. While you meditate, you should have the dream pillow resting on your lap with your hands on top of it. Focus on your question and push your magical energy and intent into the pillow. Once this has been accomplished, sleep with only this pillow. The answer to your question should be shown to you during your sleep time that night. If your question is not answered, continue to meditate on your dream pillow daily and sleep on it each night. It should not take long for you to find the answers you are looking for.

While many of the herbs we have talked about have similar magical attributes, it's important that you understand what you're working with before you proceed in using them with spells. They each hold different power and can provide you with different results. This is only a small portion of the huge variety of herbs and spells that are available to you. It is a good place to start. As you continue to grow your skills, you can move on to more intricate spells that use and an even larger variety of herbs.

Chapter 6: Herbal Remedies Vs. Prescription Medications

In this, we are going to discuss a variety of different herbal remedies. We are going to look at how herbal remedies can be more advantageous in healing than prescription medications. You will also gain valuable insight into the differences between the two.

You can use herbal remedies to help inflammation, infections, your overall immune function, neurological, and psychological disorders. There is an amazing amount of uses for herbs when it comes to healing. It is important to note that you should never completely replace modern medicine. If you are suffering from a major ailment seeking out a medical professional is important. So, while herbal remedies can help you in a huge way when it comes to your ailments, you need to always take into consideration whether or not it is important to see a doctor.

The combination of your magical practices and herbs can promote healing on a variety of levels. Healing through herbal magic is not something new. In fact, it has been around for centuries. There is basically no point throughout the time that you can't find herbal remedies being used to help heal people. With the combination of your magical practice, the healing potential is heightened immensely.

It is not uncommon for people suffering from different ailments to seek out an herbalist. This is due to the fact that they are looking for a natural solution. Unfortunately, we live in a society where pills are constantly pushed at us to help kill any issues we're having. These pills can leave us with unwanted side effects. The reason that so many people turn to herbal medicines is the fact that there are fewer side effects, and the results are easily seen. It has also been found the herbal remedies can promote faster healing that is more effective.

People also seek out herbalists due to the fact that they have quite a different demeanor than doctors. Herbalists see us as individuals. They handle our issues on a singular basis. Unfortunately, many doctors tend to look at their patients as a paycheck. Doctors also tend to look at humans as if they're all the same. Sure, we are all made of the same things, but that does not mean that our ailments should be treated the exact same way every time. Body chemistry between individuals is absolutely different, and it is important that when working on healing, this fact is recognized. Herbalists understand this and, in turn, they will pay attention to what it is that makes you, you instead of lumping you in with everyone else.

Herbal remedies are not only a more natural way of healing; they tend to be much cleaner. In today's medicine, there is a large variety of different chemicals and manmade items included. These chemicals will attack your body. Sometimes, they will be able to solve the problem; however, our bodies do not always handle this very well. It can leave you feeling worse than when you started due to the side effects that can occur.

Natural healing was extremely common in times of old. Herbal remedies were consistently used. Many people moved away from that as modern technology and medical practices assured them that their way of doing things was better. As time has moved on, many people have realized that natural healing is actually one of the better ways to go. If we can avoid putting chemicals that are unwanted into our bodies, why would we do it?

There are a lot of herbs that are still used today in Medical Sciences. This is due to the fact that the properties of herbal remedies still hold value. A great example of this is the drug aspirin. Its main ingredient comes from a shrub. It is the Spiraea plant, and aspirin will always be derived from it. This is only one of the thousands of examples of herbs still being used in modern medicine today. However, you must keep in mind that the majority of medicine used today is made from chemicals rather than plant-based ingredients.

Practitioners of herbal medicine come in a lot of different varieties. They all do basically the same thing, but they do it in different ways. Herbal medicine can help make you happier and healthier due to the healing potential in energy that herbs provide. Some of the different herbal practices are Native American herbalism, folkloric herbalism, and many others. Taking the time to look into each of them can help provide you with a clear answer as to what will fit well into your beliefs and allow you the healing that you are searching for.

At this point, we are sure you are quite aware of the major role that herbs play in magic, as well as medicine. The energy inside of these magical plants can be harnessed and help promote healing both inside and outside of your body. Whether you suffer from physical, mental, or spiritual ailments, herbs are there to help you get better.

Herbal Remedies for Common Ailments

Now that we have looked at some of the major differences between herbal remedies and modern medical practices, we're going to look more closely at some actual remedies that can be used in your life. Herbal remedies come in a plethora of different options so, finding the best one for you can be a bit difficult. Visiting an herbalist in spending time talking about the type of healing that you need is advantageous. They have a great understanding of herbs and all of their healing attributes.

The first common ailment that we're going to take a look at is inflammation. When our body sustains some sort of injury, one of its first responses is inflammation. Think of inflammation as a signal flag to our immune system. It shows our immune system that repairs need to be made. Inflammation is extremely common, and there is a plethora of different herbs that can be utilized to deal with inflammation without needing to take a pill prescribed to you by your doctor. Let's take a few moments and look at a few of the different options that you have to handle inflammation   naturally.

- **Frankincense:** The Boswellia tree produces the resin, Frankincense. It is found in Ethiopia, Somalia, the Arabian Peninsula, and India. Not only does it provide relief from inflammation, but it also helps with arthritis pain. When combined with Curcumin, also known as Turmeric, it has been found to be effective for handling issues like osteoarthritis. If you have chronic inflammation problems, you can take three to five-hundred milligrams of extract up to three times a day.

- **White Willow Bark:** White Willow bark has been used for a plethora of time to handle inflammation. It was seen being used as early as the Egyptian era. It has been found that the effects of this item are very similar to that of aspirin. It has also been noted that the side effects are decreased with white Willow bark when compared to the side effects of aspirin. If you suffer from inflammation, you can consume 240 milligrams of white Willow bark extract to handle the issue. It can also be combined with other herbs to help with issues like headaches.

- **Cat's Claw:** Found in Peru, cats claw is a Vine. People that suffer from bursitis, arthritis, or disorders of the intestines can benefit from drinking tea made with the bark of this fine. The anti-inflammatory response is that our body produces can be reduced while using this herb. It also helps keep your stomach feeling better as it protects you from gastrointestinal inflammation. Making cats claw T is simple. You'll want to use about one thousand milligrams of the bark of this vine. It should be added to eight ounces of hot water. It is important to note that you can also buy cats claw as a dried extract. You will typically want to consume forty to sixty milligrams daily to handle issues of inflammation.

It is important to note that these are only a few of the many herbs that are advantageous to help you with inflammation. You really can find natural relief for a variety of inflammatory issues. Meeting with an herbalist or discussing more natural remedies with your doctor is always a good first step before making medical decisions.

Now that we have taken a look at inflammation, we're going to move on to another common ailment. Infection happens to each and every one of us at some point in our lives. Typically, when we have an infection, we get prescribed an antibiotic such as amoxicillin or penicillin. This has helped a plethora of people overcome infectious ailments for a long period of time. While these practices are extremely effective, there are also some natural remedies to help you heal from an infection. The side effects of natural antibiotics are far less than the negative effects of prescription antibiotics. As we did before, let's take a look at some different natural remedies that can help your body handle an infection.

- **Echinacea:** From traditional healers to Native American healers, Echinacea is used to help heal wounds that have become infected. Not only that, it helps to treat infections like toxic shock syndrome and strep throat. The extract from this plant kills a variety of different types of bacteria. It has also been found to help fight against the inflammation that bacteria cause with infection. Depending on how you consume this item will depend on how much you take. Many find great success is when using it in the form of tea. Six to eight ounces of echinacea tea four times a day works well for most people. You should start drinking it as soon as you notice a sign of infection. You will likely need to consume it over the course of ten days.

- **Goldenseal:** The root of this herb is frequently dried to make a variety of different medicines. It can be used to treat urinary tract infections quite successfully. Additionally, it can help with diarrhea caused by bacteria. More often than not, people drink it in a T or swallow it in a capsule. Capsules don't tend to be as effective. Tea is absorbed into our bodies very quickly. Recently it has been found that goldenseal can be used to help with skin infections. It is important to note that this herb may interfere if you are taking other prescription medications, so it is important to talk with your doctor before starting it. It has a variety of components that are found in natural antibiotics. It is, however, not safe for pregnant women or infants to take.

There are a few other herbs out there that can help with the infection. However, these are the two most commonly used ones. The information on the other herbs is not as solid as the information on these ones. An infection can be a very serious thing so, speaking with your herbalist or doctor to ensure that you are using the right herb to handle your problem is imperative.

Keeping your immune system boosted is always a good thing. A strong immune system can help ensure that you don't get sick as frequently. Your body will be better equipped to handle things like a cold or the flu. The better your immune system is, the better you are, overall. When trying to lead a healthy life having a strong immune system is a key element. Surely, you won't be surprised to find out that there is a wide variety of herbs that can help boost your immune system. Let's take a look at some of them.

- **Oregano:** Oregano is a fantastic herb to work into your routine when you are trying to boost your immune system. It has a lot of critical vitamins that you may be lacking. These include vitamin C, a comma OK, and E. Each one of these vitamins has been proven to be beneficial to your immune system. Additionally, oregano can help with inflammation and fungal infections. Studies have found that the oils from oregano can help your body fight MRSA and listeria. When using oregano oil's, you need to be aware of some potential side effects. There are people that are allergic to it. If you have an allergy to basil, mint, sage, or lavender, you will probably want to avoid this herb. Women that are pregnant or nursing should also refrain from using oregano oil. It is not approved for use in children, and if you have any sort of disorder with bleeding, you should absolutely talk to your doctor first. It can be made into a tincture, or many prefer to use it in capsule form. If used in capsule form, three one hundred and fifty-milligram doses per day will suit your purpose.

- **Licorice Root:** Licorice root works a little bit differently. It helps with a variety of different ailments. The reason these herb works is that it boosts your adrenal glands. It also helps to handle your responses to stress. Our immune systems are connected to our adrenal system. When our bodies become stressed out, it wears down the adrenal glands and our immune systems. This can leave you susceptible to attacks that your immune system can no longer handle. So, when you support your adrenal glands, you are also supporting your immune system. The best way to promote your immune system with this herb is to make a tea out of it. The leaves of the plant can be crushed and ride to create it. You should not ingest more than six to eight ounces of tea containing licorice per day. This small amount will easily aid your adrenal glands, and in turn, your immune system.

- **Turmeric:** Turmeric is considered to be a superfood. It promotes your immune system and is full of antioxidants. It can help with inflammation, viruses, and a variety of different fungal infections. Many people find that it helps immensely with the common cold. It can also help with more serious issues like cancer or the flu. This herb is truly versatile and can help everyone lead a healthier life. Consuming this herb as a tea is very popular. You will not need a large helping of this type of tea to boost your immune system. One eight-ounce glass per day should do you just fine. When dealing with more serious issues, you will want to consult an herbalist to attain proper dosing.

Obviously, keeping your immune system in a strong state is going to be advantageous in keeping you healthy. When you have a strong immune system, fighting off- bacteria, inflammation, infection, and other issues is easier. You will recover more quickly and be back to normal life. Keep in mind that we've only given you a few looks at the many different herbs that can be used to help boost and support your immune system.

Your neurological function or brain power can also be improved with the use of herbs and herbal remedies. In fact, it is surprising to find out, but the effects the herbs can have on conditions like Alzheimer's is quite drastic. Our overall cognition is improved when we start to add different herbs to our diets. Let's look over a list of different herbs that can help improve your neural function

- **Sage:** Sage is an extremely common herb that most people already using their cooking. It has a very strong smell. It can be used to combat the effects of Alzheimer's disease. It contains a variety of different compounds that help improve neurological functions. You don't have to do anything special to consume this herb. It can be added to a variety of different food dishes. This includes things like tomato sauce and chicken. And there is no exact measurement as to how much sage you need to improve your mental functions. Eating it on a daily basis will show you reward in your levels of cognition.

- **Turmeric:** Turmeric is also fantastic when you are trying to boost your brain health. It has a variety of different effects that are beneficial. It helps to remove protein fragments from the brain, which can slow the pace of Alzheimer's disease. It also helps to stop the nerves inside your brain from breaking down. Turmeric is another ingredient that can be used in a variety of different recipes. The daily dose is not exact, but eating it frequently and making sure it is a part of your diet can help ensure your brain stays extremely healthy and alert.

- **Ginkgo-Biloba:** Ginkgo-Biloba is being used for dementia and other cognitive issues. It has been used for this purpose in an exceptionally long period of time. It is known for improving circulation and blood flow to your brain. Some of the results of testing have mixed outcomes. However, people that ingest this herb daily have noticed improved cognitive function. It has also been suggested that it helps with the declining nature of Alzheimer's Disease.

- **Lemon Balm:** Lemon balm tea has been used over the course of the centuries to help relieve symptoms of anxiety, as well as insomnia. Recently it has also been found to help height and your level of cognitive function. This tea should be consumed fairly frequently and for a longer period of time than many other medicines. Most consume it daily for at least four months. There is no harm in consuming this tea daily or even twice daily for prolonged periods of time. When this is done, the effects of Alzheimer's disease and dementia are decreased. The improvement in the level of cognitive function is quite amazing.

Fighting off ailments like dementia and Alzheimer's disease can be quite difficult. These two ailments are a major burden in not only the person suffering from it but also those that love them. Having the ability to improve cognitive function when you are suffering from one of these two issues is outstanding. There are many other herbs available that can help people who do not suffer from these types of conditions but want to improve their neurological function. There are a variety of different books and articles that can be used to provide you with this information. You can also contact an herbalist or your doctor to discuss different herbal remedies to help boost your neurological functions.

Doctors are very quick to throw anti-depressants at patients who have mental health issues. These come with a plethora of nasty side effects. They can make you feel as if you are living life in a constant haze or as if you do not care about anything at all. This is a big part of the reason that many people are turning to herbal remedies to help combat there mental or psychological issues. There are a variety of different herbs that have research to support the fact that they can reduce the symptoms of mental illness. They can be used in a variety of different ways, including baths, tinctures, cooking, and salves. Here is a look at a variety of different herbs that can help improve the symptoms of mental illness.

- **Saffron:** Saffron is used frequently as an expectorant, sedative, source for pain relief, and to combat depression. Not only is it good for treating depression, but it can also help bring calmness to your nervous system. The effects it has will reduce your level of anxiety. When compared to anti-depressants like Fluoxetine, Saffron is much more effective. It helps to relax our muscles, and in turn, helps to relax the mind. Interestingly enough, it also helps us digest food and improve appetite. This can be extremely important as many people who suffer from depression do not consume nearly enough calories to sustain their bodies.

- **Licorice:** If you are in need of an anti-depressant, anti-viral, expectorant, or an anti-inflammatory remedy that is natural licorice can be advantageous. The compounds found in licorice help to stimulate our adrenal glands. Our adrenal functions are majorly impacted by our stress levels. So, when our adrenal glands are functioning at their highest level, we will experience a reduction in depression, stress, and anxiety. A large number of mental illnesses happen due to issues with our nervous system. So, by adding licorice into your routine, you can help combat the negative symptoms of mental health issues.

- **Bacopa:** Bacopa is being used as much today as it was in the past centuries, as it is quite effective as an anti-depressant. It also allows a person better levels of focus and energy. It helps by lowering stress levels. Additionally, it helps our bodies react more positively to the stress that we come into contact with on a daily basis. Bacopa has compounds in it that increase the functionality of our brains. This is especially true in regard to our ability to process cognitively and to remember things. Many use this herb to treat anxiety on a daily basis. It has proven itself effective for those who have post-traumatic stress disorder. It is also advantageous for those suffering from memory loss, learning problems, and focus issues to consume Bacopa.

Mental illness is not something that you should take lightly. As always, getting in contact with an herbalist or your doctor is the best course of action before trying to create a regimen of herbal supplements to help with your ailments. Many of the items we have listed have proven themselves to be successful, and there are others that are equally as successful. Keep in mind that we are all wired a little bit differently, so what works for one may not work as well for another.

Magic & Herbal Remedies

All of these remedies will be quite successful on their own. It does not require magic to find the power of herbs. However, if you are looking to enhance the healing power of herbal remedies, magic into the mix is going to work out quite well for you. By tapping into the energy surrounding us, we can enhance the healing process.

Enhancing your herbal remedies with magic is not difficult. For the most part, all you will need to do is meditate over the ingredients of the remedy you are about to use. By focusing your intent and your energy into the items, they will be able to enhance the process of healing.

Adding a mantra to your meditation practice when adding power to your herbal remedy is always a good thing. There are a variety of different mantras, and it will depend on the type of healing that you are trying to perform on what you want to use.

Herbal remedies and magic practices have gone hand in hand for generations. All of your healing spells will likely involve herbs of some type. So, it is easy to see how adding magic into your remedies would work just as well. From the start of creating an herbal remedy, you should focus on positive energy and intent into every step of the process. This will provide your healing efforts with everything they need to accomplish the task at hand.

Chapter 7: Enhancing Herbal Spells

Obviously, herbs hold a great deal of power on their own. However, there are a variety of different tools that you can add to your spells to enhance the power. In this chapter, we are going to look at how candles, crystals, stones, gems, and meditation can truly add a great deal of power to any spell that you are trying to cast.

We're going to start by looking at the power of candles. Candles are used in just about every magic ritual and spell that is performed. They come in all different colors, and each color will provide you with enhanced power in a different area. You can see the use of candles in just about every culture and religion that is around   today.

Candles

When you start to look at the histories of candles in regard to magic, you will find that they are sacred. With their fire, they helped lead us out of the darkness. Candles are also associated with the dead. There are spells that revolve around candles that allow you to communicate with those that are in their afterlife, find treasure, and improve your dream states.

The exact time that candles started being used in magical practices is unknown. You can find documentation of their uses back to the times of the ancient Egyptians. In addition, they have been used throughout basically every culture and religion from the beginning of mankind.

Candle flames were looked at as a thing of mystery. People found that if they stared into the flame and entered a meditative state, they could reach different levels of consciousness. Some were able to connect with the higher powers, and others claimed to be able to look into the future.

Magical rituals involving candles are extremely common. They are used to help manifest spells for love, prophetic dreams, insight, enlightenment, removing hexes, and many other purposes. Candles truly are a major part of the magic.

Pagans have and always will use candles during their rituals. They are frequently put on altars or at the quarters of a cast circle. Frequently we see them being used at the points of the pentagram.

The color of a candle will influence a spell in different ways. Colors have their own vibrations and attributes that need to be taken into consideration if you plan on energizing an herbal spell with their influence. Most people will anoint their candles before casting a spell. Different oils are used to do this. Depending on the type of spell that you are going to cast will depend on the type of oil that you use. To anoint your candle, you simply need to rub oil into it and concentrate on the intent of your spell.

Let's take a moment and look at the different colors of candles that are available. Additionally, we will discuss the type of spells that each color is going to be best suited for. Magical work is enhanced by colored candles because of their vibration.

White candles are frequently used when somebody is casting a spell for strength. They are also fantastic for spells when you are trying to find spiritual truths. Purification or purity spells are also going to be enhanced when you burn a white candle. Many people find that they can reach deeper levels of meditation when they burn white candles during the process. Additionally, you can break curses and attract positive forces into your life with candle work using white candles.

Pink candles should be used when you are casting spells that have to do with friendship or love. Pink candles are fantastic when you are trying to reach a state of harmony within your life. They can also be used to bring calmness to your home.

Red candles should be used when you are trying to improve your physical health or your strength. Red is also the color of sexuality and passion. So, if you are looking for a boost in your love life, a red candle can help. Some people will also use red candles in protection spells.

Using orange candles can help provide you with courage. They help when you are casting spells for communication. When searching for better levels of concentration, casting spells using orange candles is advantageous. They are also fantastic when you are trying to solve problems that seemed to have no solutions. Orange candles can also be helpful when you are casting spells for the encouragement of oneself or others.

Yellow candles can help when casting spells of persuasion. They help to provide the spellcaster with higher levels of charm and confidence. If you need to enhance your memory or improve your studying skills, using an orange candle can be of great help.

Green is the color of prosperity and money. So, using green candles during spells for one of these two things will be extremely helpful. Green candles are also good when providing someone with a healing ritual. You can also use them when you are casting spells of fertility. Green is also a great color for spells associated with finding better luck.

Blue candles are quite versatile. They are fantastic to use in spells cast for spiritual or psychic awareness. People also use them when casting spells for protection while they're sleeping and peace in their everyday lives. Prophetic dreams can also come to manifestation when casting spells using blue candles.

Purple candles have a plethora of different magical uses. If you are lacking in ambition using a purple candle in your spells can help you find it. Additionally, they're great for reversing any curses that may have been cast on you or your loved ones. Purple candles are great to enhance the speed at which you heal. It also can be used to help you hold authority among a group of peers. If you are looking for the extra power to enhance any type of spell, a purple candle is never a bad idea.

While gold candles don't offer as many uses, they are quite powerful. They are fantastic when you are casting protection spells. Additionally, if you are searching for enlightenment and connection to the universe or the higher powers, using a gold candle in your spells or meditation practices will enhance the power and ease of reaching your desired outcome.

Like gold candles, silver candles don't offer a lot of versatile use. They can be used in spells to improve a person's intuition. They can also help unlock information from your subconscious mind.

Last but not least, let's talk about black candles. They can be used in spells to help reduce the impact of losing a loved one. They can also be used to remove sadness or discord from somebody's life. Black handles are great when trying to deal with negativity or negative energy that is surrounding your life or your home.

As you can see, candles by themselves play a pretty big role in the art of spellcasting. When you add candles to your herbal magic routines, the power of those spells will be enhanced greatly. This will ensure that you are able to manifest whatever outcome you are searching for. Using the proper colored candle and lighting it for the proper amount of time is important. Having spells of the herbal variety mixed with candle magic will yield great results.

Crystals, Stones, and Gems

From the time of the ancient Sumerians, crystals, stones, and gems have then regarded highly. They were found to enhance the power of spells. Regardless if you were trying to improve your health, game protection, or rid evil spirits from your life's crystals, stones, and gems can help in achieving your desired outcome. This was true way back in the day, and it continues to be true today.

Ancient Greek cultures also found that they could harness the power of crystals, stones, and gems. In fact, a lot of the words we use to name these items come from the Greek. These are only a couple of examples of where crystals, stones, and gems have played a role. Basically, every religion or culture has information in regard to the power of these three items.

There was a period of time that these important tools were pushed out of sight. It was thought that their power was that of superstition. As time moved on, experiments we're done to see if crystals, gems, and stones had any effects at all. It was surprising to find that they affected people on a physical, mental, and emotional level.

This helped to rekindle the use of crystals, stones, and gems in magical practices. Old traditions were combined with these newfound ideas, and the popularity of these items soared. Today there are many books, articles, and other works that provide teachings toward the power of using crystals in your everyday life. Crystal therapy and magic can be used to solve a variety of different problems.

It is important to note that there are some differences between crystals, stones, and gems. It is not always simple to figure out what you are looking at, so knowing these differences is important when you are trying to work on a spell. Gems are made from minerals. They are typically very rare. Gyms are pulled from the earth. From there, they are, typically, cut, and polished. Jewelry and other forms of decoration typically involve gemstones. The nature of them can be precious or semi-precious. Diamonds, emeralds, and sapphires are all examples of precious gems.

Regular stones and gemstones are different things. Standard stones will hold some power, but they're not going to be as attractive looking as gemstones. They do not have as much value monetarily nor do they hold the same kind of power that gemstones will. Regular stones can be found in nature, and their power can be utilized right away.

Crystals are a bit different from gemstones and stones. They're always in the form of a pattern. This is how they naturally occur. They are geometric in shape. The angles of the crystal are all in symmetry. Crystals are three dimensional. And the order of them is easily seen this way. You should keep in mind that crystals cannot be gems, but gems can be crystals.

Of the three categories, gemstones are the most expensive. Crystals are somewhere in between common stones and gemstones when it comes to price. This is why many people prefer to work with crystals as they fit into their budgets more easily. You can find crystals in many decorative pieces including jewelry, ambulance, and vases. When you need an extra boost of energy when casting a spell, crystals are a fantastic go-to option.

There is a massive amount of crystals, stones, and gems that are available to you. It would be impossible for us to go through each and every one. However, we're going to look at some of the most powerful and versatile options that are available to you. They can help power your spells with the extra kick you need to find true manifestation.

The first crystal that we would like to discuss is amethyst. It holds a great deal of power. You will find that this crystal is extremely spiritual. When your life is lacking peace or stability, using an amethysts power in your spells will help rid you of these burdens. It is also a good crystal to use and strong spells. During meditation, it can provide you with higher levels of energy to ensure that your focus stays on point. It also helps to promote calmness, which puts you in the correct mind frame for meditation.

Agate is a stone that is quite common. It is fantastic when you are casting strength spells. It will help you find the strength of your mind, body, and spirit. Many use it when casting spells for courage. It is also beneficial when you are trying to gain control of your emotions. Heightened emotions can make seeing the truth of a situation difficult so casting a spell with agate for a clear mind will allow you to see what is truly going on an accept those truths.

Purification spells can be heightened by using blue quartz. The type of purification, whether it is mental, emotional, or physical, does not matter. This crystal is very calming and can provide you with the words you need to communicate clearly with others.

Clear calcite also has a ton of different magical attributes. There are several different colors of calcite. Clear calcite will allow you to reach higher levels of consciousness and develop spiritually. Golden calcite can be used for spells of relaxation and to help you reach different realms.

Fire agate is a stone that many people will use in spells that are for courage. It is also extremely powerful when used in spells for protection. If you need to adjust the negative thought patterns you have recently been dealing with meditating with this stone can help reverse them. The connection this stone has with the earth is fantastic, so grounding spells will benefit when fire agate is around. The energy that comes from this stone is very calm and provides people with a sense of security.

If your life seems out of balance, casting spells while using green Jade can be helpful. This common yet powerful stone can bring peace to the tumultuous nature of life. It can also provide you with clarity of the mind, body, and soul. It can also be used in spells to bring love to your life. Many find that it also works well when you are casting spells for courage or enhanced wisdom.

A less common stone but also a highly powerful one is labradorite. If you are trying to work on your chakra system, it can help you direct energies more easily. It can allow you to find balance more quickly and this will play a role in every aspect of your life. The connection between your physical and spiritual self will be enhanced. When you are searching for a connection with the universe or higher powers through spellcasting, this stone can help.

Moonstone can help provide us with new beginnings. When performing any type of lunar magic, the use of moonstone is advantageous. If you are searching for higher levels of intuition or you are struggling with the changes that happen in life, casting spells that are aided by the power of moonstone can help correct these issues. Many people find that simply having this stone around helps to lift their spirits. It also holds the power to boost psychic abilities and help you connect with your subtle body. When working on ventures of astral projection and lucid dreaming moonstone can also be quite helpful.

As we discussed with candles, stones can add a lot of power to your herbal rituals and spells. When you combine crystals, stones, or gems to the magical workings, you are participating in their energy enhancement can be quite amazing. This is especially true with herbal magic due to the fact that all of these items come from the earth. Their lines of power are intermingled.

Getting to know and building a collection of crystals, gems, and stones are going to help give you the power you need to manifest a variety of different spells. Whether you are working on finding love, peace, prosperity, money, or other wants or desires using herbal spells mixed with crystals, stones, and gems will help to ensure that they come to fruition.

Meditation

We have discussed meditation several times throughout this book. That is due to the fact that it is such a critical element of spellcasting. Meditation should become one of your daily practice is if it is not already. The power that you can build through meditation is absolutely unreal.

When you meditate, your mind relaxes is and you have the ability to start focusing on the world around you instead of what is right in front of you. As you start to do this, you will notice that the energies surrounding you can be manipulated. You will also gain better clarity an insight into yourself and those around you when practicing meditation on a frequent basis.

Many people find time to meditate throughout the day. It can be done for a variety of different purposes. Some people meditate to find calmness or peace when their day is going less than great. Others use it to center themselves as they start to feel unbalanced. Obviously, meditation is a huge part of magical practices and should be done at just about every stage of spellcasting.

Your herbs and herbal spells all require some meditation time. This will help you to impress your intent on them. When your tools for magical rituals and spells have an intent pressed into them, it will make manifestation much easier. These herbs will absorb your purpose and then release their power to make it happen.

Some people have a hard time getting into a meditative state. For others, it comes simply and naturally. As with all things, if you struggle with meditation, in the beginning, you'll need just to be patient and continue to practice. There is a large variety of guided meditations that are available to you today. Guided meditation can make getting your head into the proper zone much easier.

Meditation is a practice that has been around for basically ever. It is a practice that will continue to be around for generations to come. This is because true enlightenment and understanding of the world will require a calm and peaceful mind, body, and soul. When we meditate on a regular basis reaching this state of calmness becomes much easier.

Chapter 8: Moon Magic

In the last chapter of this book, we are going to cover a decent amount of information in regard to full moon magic. The moon plays a role in all things on the earth. There are three bodies that are involved in the moon phases. They are the sun, earth, and moon.

The moon moves in cycles just as our lives do. We can feel the push and pull of the moon phases quite literally. This astrological body is closer to earth than any other one. It actually has quite a bit of influence over our emotions. It also has influence over the earth, including the tides.

As most people know, the moon has different lunar phases. It moves from a new moon to a full moon. There is a total of eight different moon phases. The moon always stays the same; however, how it looks to us on earth changes due to the reflection of the sun's light. Depending on the position of the sun and the moon will depend on what we see in the Night Sky. A lunar cycle lasts just under 30 days.

Each phase of the moon holds different properties. A new moon is also referred to as being in the waxing phase. It is at the beginning of the lunar cycle. When the moon and the sun come back together, and you cannot see a trace of the moon at night, this is considered a new moon. When you are trying to start a new beginning or have a new frame of mind, it is advantageous to cast spells during the new moon. The possibilities are endless. The new moon is also a fantastic time for releasing fear and setting your intentions. Trying to manifest to desires and connect with the higher powers is best suited to be done at the time of the new moon.

Right after the new moon, we enter the phase of the waxing crescent. It is a bit brighter, and it is the first step in becoming a full moon. It helps us form commitment with the intentions we laid forth at the time of the new moon. During this phase of the moon, you will need to stay determined in your intentions. It can be a time where people fall back into old patterns if they do not stay focused and the outcomes that they are working toward. There is not a lot of magical spells that people perform during this moon phase.

From a waxing Crescent, we move into the first quarter moon. This is when the moon is half full. Our plans for the future will start to unfold at this stage of the moon. You may need to recast or meditate on spells you cast at the new moon to ensure that they have the energy they need to manifest. An effort must be put forth throughout the entire spell casting process. You may cast spells to invoke new visions of your future at this stage of the lunar cycle.

After the waxing Crescent, we have the waxing gibbous. When the moon is almost full, its power intensifies. If you need to make any changes to your spell work, now is the time to do it. Many people find that this phase of the moon is stressful. Spells are getting ready to manifest, and that can bring anxiety into one's life. The best thing that you can do is stay focused and continue to meditate on your intent for your desired outcome. You may need to continuously bring energy into your home and interior life during this phase of the moon, as exhaustion can be a problem.

Now we move into the phase of the full moon. This is when we have the ability to see the entire no. Any spells cast at the new moon will be fulfilled or come to manifestation. The intentions that we set should have been focused on throughout the entire lunar cycle so that we can see the result as we stroll into the phase of the new moon. Our spells come to fruition frequently at this time of the month. When you find that your spells have come to fruition, it is important that you exude gratitude to the universe for the hard work it has helped you to accomplish.

After the full moon, there is the waning gibbous. This phase helps us to remember that we need to share our results and efforts with the world around us. Take a look at how your manifestations are helping the world around you. Meditation at this moon phase is important as it can provide you with a deeper understanding of your accomplishments and allow you to anchor yourself. Make sure to express gratitude to the higher powers in the universe during this moon cycle.

When the moon is in its last quarter phase, it is a waning half-moon. This time. Will allow our consciousness to expand. It will give us a good look at what we have created. Some people find this is a time of crisis as the end of a moon cycle is coming close. Final outcomes cannot be changed easily especially after the manifestation of spells that have already been cast. When you are trying to see the bigger picture in life, this is the time of the moon cycle to do it. Prophecies and visions are almost always born during this time of the month.

The last moon phase is called the waning Crescent. This is the end of the entire cycle, and it is the time for you to let go of any negativity that has crept into your life. You are getting ready to enter a new moon and the stage of new beginnings. Many people find that receiving messages from spirits and higher powers is much easier at this point because the veil between realities is much thinner.

Most people prefer to work with magic during the new moon or the full moon. Keep in mind it is oftentimes best too cast your spells and intentions during the new moon so that they can manifest with the energy of the full moon. Some people will work with moon magic throughout all of the phases; however, it is most common to perform spells or rituals on the new moon or the full moon.

You can work through any magical spells by the power of the moon, but some spells will work better than others. Moon magic helps too open our memories and route us to what is most important. It connects us to our feelings, as well as the higher powers of the universe. It can help us understand how to care better for ourselves and for others.

Whether you are working with crystals, stones, gems, candles, or herbs, all spells can be cast during the lunar phases. Some of these items are directly associated with the moon which will make them more powerful tools when casting spells under a new or full moon. There are stones, crystals, gems, candles, and herbs that are associated with the son. Obviously, casting these spells with items related to the sun is not going to work as well if you try and do them at night.

Now that we have discussed a variety of pieces of information in regard to the phases of the moon, let's move on. There are a variety of different things that you can accomplish during the phase of the full moon. Let's take a look at some different spells that will easily manifest when you cast them during a full moon.

If you have been having issues with your finances, bringing money into your life is easily accomplished by casting spells for it during the full moon. The energy of the full moon is at its highest point. This can supercharge wealth or financial spells. Many people find their greatest successes in spells for financial gain when they do them on this phase of the moon. This is due to the fact that energy levels are in abundance and you'll be able to hone in your intention and supercharge the energy that flows through yourself and your magical tools.

Most people find a full moon to be extremely romantic. Due to this fact, it makes it an excellent time for casting love spells. If you are having any sort of emotional turmoil the time to cast spells to remove it is during the full moon. Love spells cast at the full moon can allow us to open ourselves to romantic love and to experience all that life has to offer. Adding candles, herbs, and crystals to your love spells or love charms can make them truly powerful. Focus on your affirmations or mantras to manifest the love that you have been searching for.

The full moon is also a great time to add energy to your tools. During the time of the full moon letting your crystals, stones, or gems bathed in the light of it can add an extreme amount of energy to them. When you go to cast spells with these crystals, stones, or gems, their power enhancement will be easily noticed. Manifestation will also become easier once you have empowered your crystals with the strength of the moon.

If you have noticed negative energies around your home, clearing them during the time of the full moon is advantageous. The magical energies that are around are fantastic for casting blessings or protection spells in your space. Obviously, setting your intention is extremely important in removing unwanted or negative energy that may be lingering around you or your home.

Many people find that the most accurate readings of tarot cards occur at the full moon. If you are interested in getting a glimpse of the future, reading your tarot during the full moon is advantageous. The power of the moon helps to provide insight into the prophecies of the future. You do not necessarily need to read your own tarot cards. Finding a trusted tarot card reader on the full moon can result in excellent information into where your life is headed.

The full moon provides us with the most light we will ever get during the time of darkness. If you are trying to find clarity in a difficult situation or shine a light on a subject casting spells of insight during the full moon will provide you with the best outcomes. Many people like to cast their divination spells at this time since true insight can be found by the light of the full moon. Your magical power will be enhanced during the full moon, and therefore your intentions will come to manifestation more easily.

We all have struggled throughout our daily lives. They can be seen with health issues, relationships, and work. If you need to cast spells to rid any sort of negativity from your life, the full moon is the time to do it. Many people participate in banishing rituals during the full moon because it can provide the type of power that is needed for these spells to come to fruition. There are some very easy spells that can be done. Let's take a look at one.

A simple ritual for banishing would be too right down on a blank piece of white paper whatever it is in life that is burdening you. Roll the piece of paper away from you so that it looks like a small scroll. Seal it with wax or a small piece of twine. From here, you will place it in a jar and cover it with salt from the sea. It is important to note that you should fill the entire jar. Place a feather that was found in nature on Top of the salt and then seal the jar. You will need to hold on to this jar for three moon cycles, and then you'll want to bury the salt and feather in the earth and burn the scroll. After burning the scroll, you will feel the burdens that were kept inside, lift from your spirit.

As with all things, this is only a look at the many different types of spells and rituals that can be cast during the full moon. The options are truly endless. Full moon magic can be extremely powerful. You should always start with the basics before trying harder spells or rituals as the outcomes may be what you intended them to be.

We all feel the power of the full moon from the time that we are small children. It affects us on a great level. During magical practices, the power that it provides is truly astonishing. If you have never worked on full moon magic, you will be quite surprised by how it feels as you work through your spellcasting practice this is. Group spellcasting is also quite powerful during the full moon. Once you move on to intermediate or advanced level spells, working with the full moon will be even more amazing. This takes time, study, practice, and effort. However, once you have invested in learning, it is amazing what you can manifest during the full moon.

Conclusion

Thank you for making it through to the end of *Wicca Herbal Magic*, let's hope it was informative and able to provide you with all of the tools you need to achieve your goals whatever they may be.

The next step is to start growing, collecting, and storing a variety of different magical herbs. You can purchase some from a local market or greenhouse to get you started. Obviously, growing your own herbs is always the most advantageous way to use them for magical purposes. You will be able to provide them with positive energy and intent from the moment they are planted.

Working with herbs is not difficult, but it does take practice. With patience and time, you can become very familiar with a variety of herbs and their magical attributes. With this knowledge, you will be able to participate in spells, rituals, magical baths, and other Wiccan practices confidently.

Herbs are great for spellcasting, as well as healing. Many ailments can be treated easily with herbs, which will allow you to avoid the harmful chemicals that are frequently found in pharmaceuticals. This can lead to a happier and healthier life. There are a time and a place for more modern medicines; however, natural remedies are always a great way to go. Don't forget to gain insight from an herbalist or your doctor before trying to heal yourself or others with herbal remedies.

Working with crystals, stones, gems, and candles can add great power to your spells. Remember to take your time in spellcasting ventures as rushing never did anyone any good. Keep practicing and focusing, and you will easily be able to see the power of herbal magic.

Finally, if you found this book useful in any way, a review on Amazon is always appreciated!

CPSIA information can be obtained
at www.ICGtesting.com
Printed in the USA
BVHW041919050421
604248BV00024B/479